BookLife
freedom
Readers

T0015663

CHAMPIONS
of the
JUNGLE

By Madeline Tyler

BookLife
PUBLISHING

©2022
BookLife Publishing Ltd.
King's Lynn
Norfolk, PE30 4LS

All rights reserved.
Printed in Poland.

A catalogue record for
this book is available from
the British Library.

ISBN: 978-1-80155-141-0

Written by:
Madeline Tyler

Edited by:
Emilie Dufresne

Designed by:
Drue Rintoul

Photo Credits

All images are courtesy of Shutterstock.com. With thanks to Getty Images, Thinkstock Photo and iStockphoto. Throughout – Cocos.Bounty. Front Cover&1 – apple2499, CWIS, Anan Kaewkhammul, Milan M, Elnur. 2–3 – Teo Tarras, PRANEE JIRAKITDACHAKUN. 4–5 – Cristi Popescu, Ondrej Prosicky. 6–7 – Frank McClintock, Damsea, nattanan726. 8–9 – Atthapol Saita, Glenn Young, Enrique Aguirre, Travel Stock. 10–11 – jeep2499, Daniel_Ferryanto, Sanit Fuangnakhon. 12–13 – Jukka Jantunen, Shutterranger. 14–15 – mark higgins, Misbachul Munir, LeonP. 16–17 – Jonah Goh, Andreas Gradin, nattanan726. 18–19 – LABETAA Andre, Patrick K. Campbell, SachinSubran. 20–21 – Jiri Hrebicek, Eric Isselee, Marc Lechanteur, Vladimir Wrangel. 22–23 – Lori Jaeski, Purino, Darren Baker, Denis Kuvaev.

CONTENTS

BookLife
freedom
Readers

IN THE JUNGLE

Jungles are tropical forests. This means they are very hot and wet. Some animals live at the tops of the trees, some animals live on the jungle floor, and some animals live somewhere in between!

WHAT MAKES AN ANIMAL CHAMPION?

Animal champions don't always have to be the biggest, fastest, or strongest animals around. They are champions because of the things they can do or the ways that they live. Let's meet the animal champions that call the jungle their home!

THREE-TOED SLOTH

Champions of Camouflage

Sloths are some of the slowest animals on Earth. Sloths move so slowly that algae grows on them. This may not sound good, but it helps them camouflage against the green trees of the jungle. This means it is hard to see them.

Sloths spend most of their lives up in the trees. Their long claws help them hold onto branches. Sloths can even sleep while holding onto trees. This is useful because they can spend up to 20 hours a day sleeping!

JAGUAR

Champion of the Big Bite

You may think that most cats are afraid of water, but these big cats love swimming. Jaguars use this skill to hunt animals in the water. Jaguars have very strong teeth — they can bite through caimans and turtle shells!

Jaguars are also great at climbing trees. There are lots of trees in the jungle, so jaguars can climb up high to hide and to hunt.

ORANGUTAN

Champion of Strong Swings

The orangutan is the largest mammal that lives in trees. A mammal is a type of animal with warm blood, a backbone and that makes milk. Orangutan's long, strong arms make it easy to swing from branch to branch.

Orangutans are very clever and are closely related to humans. They stay dry in the wet jungle by making nests within the trees and using leaves as umbrellas. Orangutan means 'person of the forest' in a language called Malay.

AFRICAN FOREST ELEPHANT

Champion of Pooing

It can sometimes be hard to spot African forest elephants, so scientists make careful guesses about how many elephants there are by counting the elephants' poos!

The poo of African forest elephants is very important for helping the rainforest grow. Some trees grow better when an African forest elephant eats their seeds and then poos them out!

CHIMPANZEE

Champion of Clever Eating

Chimpanzees are very clever animals. They use sticks and branches to get insects from inside trees and logs. This means they can get food that some other animals may not be able to find.

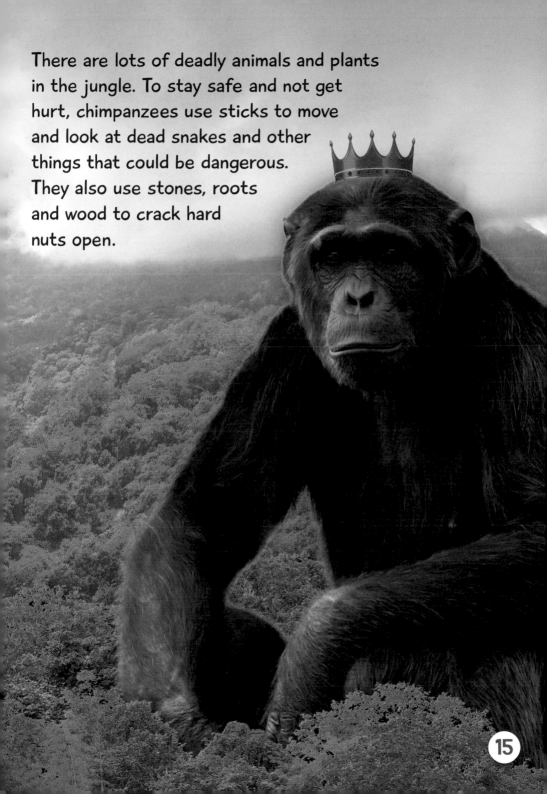

There are lots of deadly animals and plants in the jungle. To stay safe and not get hurt, chimpanzees use sticks to move and look at dead snakes and other things that could be dangerous. They also use stones, roots and wood to crack hard nuts open.

MALAYAN TAPIR

Champion of Sniffing out Smells

Malayan tapirs have a very good sense of smell. They wee on jungle pathways so that other Malayan tapirs can sniff it and find their way to feeding and drinking areas.

Swimming is a great way to cool off in the hot jungle, and tapirs are very good at it! Their snouts are good for smelling, but they also use them as a snorkel while swimming underwater.

GREEN ANACONDA

Champion of the Surprise Attack

Green anacondas are very good hunters. They are mostly nocturnal, which means they sleep during the day and hunt at night. This means it is harder for them to be seen.

A green anaconda's eyes and nostrils are on the top of its head. This allows it to hide underwater and wait for prey to come by, before taking it by surprise and attacking!

OKAPI

Champion of Not Getting Wet

Okapis have fur that is perfect for the jungle. It's very oily, so the water slides right off it, just like a raincoat. This keeps them dry on rainy days.

Okapis have long tongues that are great for grabbing and holding food. An okapi uses its tongue to pull leaves off trees and put them into its mouth.

BECOMING A CHAMPION

Let's see what we humans can use to be champions of the jungle! Face paint and camouflaged clothes will help you hide like a sloth. Shoes with good grip could help you climb like an orangutan.

A raincoat will keep you dry like an okapi.
Goggles and a snorkel will help you swim
like a green anaconda.

QUESTIONS

1: How many hours a day can a sloth spend sleeping?

2: What do orangutans use to stay dry in the jungle?
  a) Raincoats
  b) Rocks
  c) Leaves

3: When do green anacondas sleep?

4: Can you list any other jungle animals that do weird or amazing things?

5: If you could turn into an animal for one day, which animal would it be?